MW01503596

Original title:

Walking My Dog, or Being Dragged on Ice

Author: Lucas Harrington

ISBN HARDBACK: 978-9916-94-170-6

ISBN PAPERBACK: 978-9916-94-171-3

Whiskers and Wintertime Wishes

Whiskers twitch in the frosty air,
Paws dance lightly, a fluffy affair.
Snowflakes swirl, a chilly tease,
Chasing dreams with the greatest of ease.

Hot cocoa waits on the kitchen shelf,
But it's catnip snow that he loves best himself!
Pouncing high on a mound of white,
Wintertime wishes in pure delight.

The Art of Sliding Under Paws

Sliding on ice is a kitty's delight,
With a graceful leap, she takes flight.
But oops! Down she goes in a twist,
Fluff and fur in a snowy mist.

Socks flying off, I can't help but cheer,
As her furry face meets the cold out here.
With each little slip, she becomes a star,
Winter ballet, who knew she'd go far?

A Tug-of-War on an Icy Canvas

Two cats pulling on a scarf with pride,
One wins, one loses, it's a snowy ride.
Oh, what a spectacle, it's pure feline fun,
Laughing and panting, till the battle's done.

A tussle here, a tussle there,
Claws gently dancing in a frosty air.
Victory claimed with a mighty purr,
As the other one grumbles in muffled stir.

Steps of Glee in a Glacial Playground

Snowball fights in a glacial ground,
Kittens tumbling, laughter all around.
Each snowy mound a fortress grand,
In the glacial playground, they make their stand.

Paws in the air, snowflakes on nose,
Zooming past where the chilly wind blows.
They hold their heads high, with such playful glee,
In this winter wonderland, forever free.

Slipping Through a Sparkling Wonderland

The snowflakes twirl like dancers bright,
I skate on ice, oh what a sight!
With fancy moves, I take a chance,
Then land right on my rear, a comical dance.

The trees sparkle like they've been bedazzled,
While I struggle not to be too frazzled.
My friends all laugh, oh how they tease,
As I cling to a snowman, begging, "Please!"

A Dance on Frosty Pavement

I strut my stuff on icy ways,
Thinking I'm cool, in winter's haze.
With every step, a little slip,
I perform my very own winter trip!

My dance partner? A wayward cat,
Who pounces on me like we're in combat.
Together we spin, slip, and spin some more,
On frosty pavement, we just can't score.

Canine Curiosity Amidst the Cold

My dog runs wild through winter's white,
Chasing snowflakes with all his might.
He sniffs the air, then takes a leap,
And face-plants hard in a snowdrift deep.

With a shake and a wiggle, he's back in the game,
Pawing at snow like it's a wild flame.
He digs for treasures only he can see,
While I just ponder, "What could it be?"

Frozen Trails and Furry Friends

We trek through trails where snowflakes fall,
My pals and I share laughs, and a snowball brawl.
With cheeks bright red from the chilly air,
We giggle and slide, without a care.

But as we race down a slippery slope,
One shoe flies off—oh, where is my hope?
Wrapped in laughter, we stumble and shout,
In this frosty world, there's never a doubt.

Frayed Leashes and Frostbitten Toes

A leash that's frayed, a pup that's bold,
Chasing after snowflakes, bright and cold.
Frostbitten toes, they dance and prance,
While I sip cocoa, missing my chance.

My dog has swagger, thinks he's a star,
But slips on ice, oh dear, there you are!
He shakes it off, with style and glee,
While I just laugh, it's all meant to be.

Whispers of Winter in a Dog's World

The snowflakes whisper secrets low,
As pups in jackets strut to and fro.
They bark at snowmen, full of pride,
While I trip over, my frozen stride.

Winter's a time for snuggles and play,
But first, we must shovel before the day.
Paws in the snow, they leave a trail,
Of frozen chaos, that never goes stale.

Canine Chronicles of Chilly Nights

In the depths of night, when it's icy and dark,
My dog dreams of chasing a magical spark.
He snores so loud, like a thunderous roar,
I ponder if dogs can have dreams for sure.

Chilly nights call for warm beds inside,
But my pup thinks the couch is a thrilling ride.
With paws on the pillows, he claims his throne,
While I just wonder, 'Where's my space gone?'

Footprints of Friendship on Frozen Paths

Walking together on icy trails,
We leave behind our snowy tales.
Paw prints and footprints side by side,
In this frozen world, friendships abide.

Through frosty mornings and chilly nights,
Each step we take, our laughter ignites.
Dogs and their humans, a bond so true,
In a winter wonderland, just me and you.

Joyrides on a Blanket of White

Snowflakes dance with glee,
All the trees are dressed in white.
Sledding down the hill so free,
Laughing 'til we lose our sight.

Hot cocoa spills on my jeans,
Marshmallows float like little boats.
Winter's magic in the scenes,
As we bounce in fluffy coats.

Snowmen wear a wobbly hat,
Stick arms waving in delight.
Please beware of that big cat,
He thinks snowballs are a bite!

With cheeks red and spirits high,
We'll frolic until day is done.
Underneath the big, blue sky,
Winter days are all just fun.

Fluffy Hearts in a Winter's Hold

Winter's here with fuzzy mittens,
Snuggling up, I feel the warmth.
Outside, all the snowflakes whittlin',
Inside, hot drinks keep us calm.

Snowball fights afoot and frosty,
My nose is red, my toes amiss.
Together, we are all so costly,
Laughter shared in blissful bliss.

Cats in boots chase sheets of ice,
Dogs in sweaters strut and prance.
Snowflakes glitter, oh so nice,
Pets join in the winter dance!

Fluffy hearts amidst the snow,
With every giggle, joy ignites.
In this season, love will grow,
Winter cheer, our hearts' delights.

Whimsy Underneath the Icy Veil

Penguins slide and strut around,
On ice, they slip and take a dive.
With each tumble, laughter's found,
Winter's jesters, oh so alive!

Icicles hang like pointy teeth,
Nature's ornament, oh so grand.
Beware of the frosty wreath,
Used as a frisbee in hand.

Snowflakes fall with little quirks,
Each one unique, who would have thought?
Winter games for all the jerks,
While sipping cocoa, feeling fraught.

Under the stars, we all join in,
Making memories in the night.
To us, the snow will always win,
Whimsy twinkles, shining bright.

The Glacial Gambol

Here we go on icy schmooze,
Gliding past the frozen trees.
Chilly air, but we won't snooze,
While the cold wind laughs and frees.

Sliding down the snowy slopes,
Airborne laughs, and squeals of glee.
We'd be stars in winter's hopes,
Snowflakes catch our joyful spree.

Icicles sharpen like a knife,
Goblins lurking 'round to play.
Choose your battles in this life,
Or the snow will lead you astray!

With frosty cheeks and belly laughs,
We'll trudge home through winter's mist.
In our hearts, the warmth still halves,
Until the summer sun gets kissed.

Celebrating the Chill with a Companion

When winter arrives with its shivers and shakes,
I cozy up close, the warmth that it makes.
With hot cocoa in hand, we sit by the fire,
Just me and my buddy, what else could inspire?

We watch movies and laugh, in our comfy, warm den,
With popcorn explosions, oh, what a zen!
He steals all the blankets, but who needs a sheet?
His furry warmth wraps me, an infinite treat.

With snowflakes a-dancing, outside they do play,
We watch from the window, our own cabaret.
He snorts when he dreams, it's a symphony sweet,
Who needs a chill solo when you have this beat?

So here's to the cold, and our snuggly delight,
To laughter and warmth that makes everything right.
With cookies and stories, we make quite the splash,
Celebrating the chill, with love that won't clash!

Muzzles Raised to the Icy Sky

Pugs wear coats, they strut with pride,
In a world of frost, their charm won't slide.
A shivering chihuahua, wrapped up tight,
Barks at the snowflakes, oh what a sight!

The husky thinks he's a mighty wolf,
While the Pomeranian hides in a shelf.
With snouts up high, they greet the chill,
Even if walking means conquering a hill!

Navigating Nippy Neighborhoods

The dachshund's long, he leads the way,
While terriers chase shadows—what do they say?
A squirrel's on guard, he's swinging by,
With acorn armor and a watchful eye.

Pavement turns to ice, it's a slippery dance,
Each pup takes a tumble, not one has a chance.
They look back at us, tails high with glee,
Snow angels in motion, fully carefree!

The Silhouette of Joy on a White Canvas

A beagle bounds in deep snowdrifts wide,
With ears flapping wildly, join the ride!
Each leap paints laughter in frosty air,
As snowballs explode, no worry or care.

Golden retrievers dig with delight,
While poodles look fancy, snow hats pure white.
In laughter, they frolic, each paw leaves a trace,
Their joy on a canvas, we can all face.

Paws and Patterns in the Snow

Big paws make prints like a cake gone wrong,
Little paws scatter, all singing a song.
Each wagging tail creates a new hue,
Art in the snow, every dog's point of view.

From circles to zigzags, it's a puppy parade,
While cats watch in winter, slightly dismayed.
With noses to ground, they create a scene,
In a world of white, they reign supreme!

Paws Dancing on the Demise of Winter

As winter wanes, the paws take flight,
They twirl and leap in the soft sunlight.
No more snowbanks to trip or fall,
Just frolic and play, they'll have a ball.

The frostbite tales they now forget,
With every bounce, a playful duet.
Socks on their paws, oh what a sight,
Dancing on ice? Oh, what a delight!

Snowmen wobble as they jog by,
Chasing the birds that flutter and fly.
With a wink and a bark, they send spring cheer,
Paws pirouetting, winter's end is near!

So here's to the pups that shimmy and shake,
Leaving behind the cold winter ache.
With tails all wagging, it's quite the scene,
Paws dancing merrily, all happy and keen!

Frosty Fables and Playful Paws

In the land of frost, where the snowflakes drift,
Paws tell tales with a comedic twist.
A fox in boots danced right by,
While a snowman tried not to cry.

A rabbit wore earmuffs too big,
Singing a tune that was quite a jig.
Chasing a snowball, he'd trip and fall,
Rising again, he'd laugh through it all.

The crafty crows plotted mischief anew,
Dropping snowflakes like confetti, woohoo!
With every flap, they'd quack and tease,
As dogs chased wagging tails in the breeze.

So gather 'round for these frosty fables,
Where laughter and joy dance on tables.
With playful paws and tales so bright,
We'll celebrate winter 'til the summer light!

Tales of Slippery Escapades

One fine winter, the pups took a chance,
On icy sidewalks, they'd prance and dance.
With a slip, a slide, and a hilarious yell,
They'd spin like ballerinas, oh so swell!

A gourmet treat fell from a kid's hand,
But catching it proved quite unplanned.
Paws slipped and skidded in a furball race,
Trying to outpace the melting ice space.

Moments of chaos, a whirl in the snow,
They crash into bushes, laughing aglow.
With nibbles and giggles, they roll around,
In tales of escapades, pure joy is found.

As the sun sets low on this fun-filled spree,
The pups share stories for all to see.
They met slippery mischief with joyful shouts,
And winter's magic, without a doubt!

Overcoming the Chill with Unbridled Joy

When winter's grip tightens every day,
The pups find laughter in their own way.
With bright woolly hats perched on their heads,
They pop out of snowdrifts, jump out of beds.

The snowflakes fall like a waltzing band,
While puppies frolic, they'll make a grandstand.
Rolling in snow, their barks fill the air,
With icy resolve, they banish despair.

In hops and skips, they soar high and low,
Chasing their tails, ah, what a show!
Overcoming the chill with barks full of cheer,
They embrace every moment, winter's premiere.

So here's to the pups, so lively and free,
Spreading their joy like a wild jubilee.
With every leap, winter fades to a dream,
In unbridled joy, they create their own theme!

The Quest for the Perfect Sniff

I wander through the grassy park,
My nose a compass, my tail a spark.
A sniff of sunshine, a whiff of grass,
Each scent a treasure, none can surpass.

The mailman comes, a whiff of dread,
I sniff his shoes, then run like a lead.
An old shoe's scent, a mystery old,
This is the saga of sniffs to behold!

Socks in the laundry, oh, what a find!
A fragrance of chaos, wildly combined.
The perfect sniff is my noble quest,
I'll sniff till I find it, I'll never rest!

So here I roam, with nose to the ground,
In pursuit of the smells that astound.
With every sniff, my heart takes wing,
In this olfactory dance, I'm the king!

Ribbons of Ice and Spirited Leaps

The ice appears, like a glassy dream,
I zoom and slide, I'm a fuzzy beam.
On ribbons of ice, I twirl and glide,
With paws a-paddle, I can't decide!

A leap and a flop, I tumble down,
A furry acrobat with a silly frown.
With every slip, giggles abound,
I'm the clumsy prince in the snowy crown!

The snowflakes kiss my wiggly nose,
As I bound and bounce in delightful pose.
Each spirited leap brings laughter and cheer,
In this icy ballet, I've nothing to fear!

So watch me dance on this frosty stage,
With ribbons of ice, I'll never age.
In winter's grip, I frolic with zest,
In each crazy leap, I'm simply the best!

Furry Enthusiasm Meets Winter's Grip

The winter air is cold, oh dear!
But here comes fur, full of cheer.
With fur-lined boots and wagging tails,
We dash and slide, as fun prevails!

Snowballs tossed like furry missiles,
We bounce and bark amidst the whistles.
Puppy pals in a fluffy race,
Winter's grip brings a furry embrace!

The chilly breeze, it makes me sneeze,
Yet I romp and roll with playful ease.
With snowflakes flying, my heart takes flight,
Winter's a party, a pure delight!

So bring on the cold, the frost, the chill,
With furry enthusiasm, I've got the skill.
In winter's grip, we joyfully run,
With wagging tails, we're having fun!

Navigating the Slippery Dream

A shiny world, oh what a sight!
Slippery roads, my paws take flight.
I dance like a cloud, all fluffy and bright,
In this slippery dream, everything feels right.

Round and round, I spin with glee,
As I slide and glide, just like a jubilee.
Squeaky toys call from the snow-draped land,
I'm the king of the slips, here to take a stand!

But wait! What's this? A tumble and roll,
Oh dear! I've lost my control!
With legs akimbo and nose in the air,
I'll conquer this dream, it's only fair!

So here I go, on this wild ride,
In navigating dreams, I've got nothing to hide.
With laughter and joy, I revel in play,
In this slippery dream, I'll stay all day!

Dragging Dreams Through Snowdrifts

I dreamed of warm beaches in the snow,
But all I got was ice, don't you know?
My toes are frozen and my socks are wet,
I'll trade my dreams for a warm baguette.

I tried to slide, ended in a flop,
Face-planted hard, oh, what a drop!
My snowman looks like a lopsided blob,
With buttons crooked, it's quite the job.

Chasing snowflakes, I danced like a fool,
But they keep melting, breaking the rule.
Now I'm stuck sliding on each icy patch,
Like a penguin in a nice coat, what a catch!

So here I am, with my dreams all frosted,
My hot cocoa's cold, and my laughter's losted.
Next year I'll dream of a place with sun,
But for now, I'll slide, it's still kind of fun!

A Journey Through a Wonderland of Ice

In a land of frost where snowflakes play,
I tripped on my boots, oh, what a day!
With colors of winter all shimmering bright,
I thought I was graceful—what a silly sight!

A penguin waddles, steals my hot drink,
While I stand there shivering, unable to think.
Snowmen gather for a winter parade,
And I am the only one feeling dismayed.

Snow angels flutter, I try to compete,
But all I create is just a cold seat.
With ice and giggles, I stumble around,
While the rabbits just chuckle without making a sound.

This snowy wonderland is quite absurd,
I'm losing the battle, it's just too blurred.
But laughter is plenty, so I'll take my chance,
And slide through the winter in a slip-sliding dance!

Barking at the Blustery Sky

My dog barks loud at clouds way up high,
As if they're plotting, oh my oh my!
With fluffs of white and a grumpy frown,
Every gust of wind makes him chase them down.

He leaps at shadows, runs from his tail,
Going for broke, leaving a snowy trail.
I try to catch him, but he's just too fast,
Bounding in snowdrifts, oh, such a blast!

The trees seem to giggle, branches shake too,
While my pup is convinced he can sway them like dew.
A heroic bark as the tree cries back,
And we're lost in the game, no thought for the slack.

Oh, blustery sky, with your swirling delight,
You're the perfect foe for our snowy fight.
We'll bark and dance till the sun fades away,
In this frosty, funny, dog-filled ballet!

A Flurry of Paws and Tail-wags

In a whirlwind of snow, my dog spins around,
His tail is a propeller, oh what a sound!
Paws flailing wildly, he's a furry blur,
Chasing the flakes with a joyful stir.

Each leap is a classic, each wiggle a dance,
He prances and pounces, oh isn't he a chance?
His coat's all white with little mud streaks,
And winter's his playground, it's laughter he seeks.

Snowballs and snowflakes, a dog's perfect day,
With wags and barks, in a frosty ballet.
As he rolls in the drifts, a snow-dog parade,
My heart warms with giggles—joy never fades.

So let's toss a few balls, let the laughter fly,
In a flurry of paws, under this gray sky.
With every wild moment, I cherish the cheer,
For winter's a treasure when my pup is near!

The Unruly Companion on Slippery Paths

My dog decided to run, not walk,
On the icy ground, it's quite the jolt.
With paws a-flying, he took a spin,
While I just stood there, trying not to grin.

He leaped and bounded, oh what a sight,
Chasing his tail with all his might.
I yelled, 'Slow down!' but it was too late,
He crashed into snow, oh what a fate!

With fur all frosted and humor galore,
We both hit the trail, laughing more and more.
Next time I'll bring a sled or a chair,
For slippery paths and his wild flair!

So here's to the pup, my slippery mate,
Who turns every walk into a date with fate.
With snowflakes swirling and laughter loud,
My unruly companion makes me proud!

Sledding Through a Winter Wonderland

Down the hill we go, me and my pup,
On a sled that's barely holding up.
With a bark and a yip, he leaps in glee,
As we sail through the trees, the world's ours, you see!

He's in the lead, acting like a pro,
With ears flapping wildly like they're in the show.
I holler, 'Faster!' as we zoom down fast,
But the sled hits a bump, and we're outclassed!

We tumble and roll, what a glorious crash!
Snow flies around us in a dazzling splash.
With snow on our noses, we both just laugh,
Winter's a joyride, it's our favorite path!

So, here's to the sleds and the wintry fun,
With my furry friend, the world's got a run.
Through snow-draped hills, where memories blend,
Sledding together, the best time we spend!

Frosty Whiskers and Twinkling Snowflakes

In the frosty air, my pup prances proud,
With whiskers all frozen, he stands out in the crowd.
Snowflakes a-dancing, they flutter and fall,
While he tries to catch them, what a curious ball!

He sneezes at flakes, which makes me chuckle,
Running in circles, ready to snuggle.
With a wag of his tail and a playful bark,
He dives into snow, leaves a big, happy mark!

His coat all white, like a frosted cake,
Joyful and silly, for laughter's sake.
I toss him a snowball, oh, what a sight!
Frosty whiskers smiling, we play through the night!

As the stars twinkle softly above our heads,
We chase winter's magic where laughter spreads.
With frosty adventures in the moon's soft glow,
A dog and his human, creating the flow!

Canine Pirates in a Sea of Ice

Ahoy there matey, my dog leads the pack,
With a scarf for a flag, there's no looking back.
A swashbuckling dog on this icy terrain,
Searching for treasures and jellybean grain!

He barks at the gulls, 'They're after our loot!'
In the frosty sea, he parts like a brute.
Sliding and gliding, his paws make a splash,
While I take a tumble, oh what a crash!

The snow drifts are mountains, the icebergs are tall,
With my pirate pup, we're having a ball.
He finds a lost mitten, a true hidden gem,
With a growl and a wag, he claims it for him!

Around us, the world is a wintry maze,
In our imaginations, we're lost in a craze.
Together we sail through this sea of ice,
A pair of fierce pirates, oh, isn't it nice!

Adventuring Through a Crystal Maze

In a maze made of glass, I tripped on my shoe,
With every wrong turn, I yelled, "What's new?"
Reflections of me, in a wide funny dance,
I laughed at my shadow and offered it a chance.

Puzzles of ice, with a riddle or two,
I solved one, but it whispered, "Who are you?"
Chasing my tail like a confused puppy,
In this crystal conundrum, I might get grumpy.

A slippery slope, I took a big slide,
Landed in a fountain—oh what a pride!
Glistening water splashed right in my face,
Who knew a maze could be such a fun place?

At last, I emerged with a smile so bright,
With crystals and giggles, what a sheer delight!
Every twist, every turn, was a game I could play,
In this sparkling maze, I would happily stay!

Frigid Journeys with a Fluffy Navigator

My fluffy dog guides me through snowbanks so deep,
While I slip and cry, he trots like a sheep.
With paws made of fluff and a nose cold as ice,
He snickers at me—oh, isn't he nice?

We journey through winter, with snowflakes that dance,
Every time I run, he gives me a glance.
His tail's a warm flag in the blizzard's tough fight,
While I'm crying, "Fluffy, it's not day nor night!"

Chasing our shadows in the moon's gentle glow,
He leaps higher than me, as if it's a show.
My fluffy navigator, through winter's fine hug,
Reminds me that snow's just a reason to mug!

So here's to the cold and my furry best friend,
In frigid adventures, our laughter won't end!
With sips of hot cocoa and cuddles so tight,
We'll conquer the frost with joy and delight!

Tugging at the Heartstrings in the Snow

Snowflakes do dance, as I trip on a hill,
With every small tumble, I giggle at will.
My heartstrings are tugged by the snow's soft embrace,
Each flurry a tickle, all over my face.

A snowman I built with a wobbly grin,
Oh dear, it fell down with a really loud spin.
Its carrot nose flew and landed nearby,
As I howled with laughter, watching it fly!

My friends joined in with snowballs and cheer,
We made a huge mess, but we didn't care, dear!
Tugging at heartstrings wrapped tight all around,
In laughter and joy, our friendship is found.

As the sun sets low and the snow starts to glow,
We gather close 'round with hot cocoa in tow.
With each sugary sip, our hearts feel so light,
In the cold winter's snows, we shine oh so bright!

Chasing Dreams on Glistening Ice

On frozen lakes where the brave come to glide,
I tried to be graceful but went off to the side.
With dreams of a skater, I aim for pure fame,
Instead, I'm the poster for "How Not to Game!"

The ice was a mirror but I had no flair,
A spin turned to tumble, my dignity bare.
The crowd was now laughing—oh sweet irony!
Chasing my dreams? Just chasing pizza for me!

But with every bad slip, I learned how to slide,
Each wobble and shake became part of the ride.
Falling was fun, like a child's silly game,
In this icy adventure, I'll never feel shame.

So here's to the glimmers that light up the night,
To chasing our dreams and giving them flight.
With laughter and falls, joy flows just like ice,
In the dance of the skater— oh, isn't it nice?

Petals of Joy on a Frosty Path

Frosty flowers in a field,
Petals shiver, but won't yield.
I tiptoe past, with boots on tight,
Slipping once, oh what a sight!

Giggles echo through the air,
As I dodge the icy glare.
Each step a dance, a balmy game,
Nature laughs, it's all the same!

Snowflakes tease with chilly flair,
Frolicking without a care.
Joyful skipping, what a blast,
Forget the cold, let's have a blast!

With frosty fun, we'll take our time,
In this winter wonder rhyme.
While petals laugh beneath the chill,
We'll chase the joy, it's such a thrill!

Spinning in Circles on a Chill Day

Round and round, I twirl and spin,
Chilly cheeks and frosty chin.
The world around, a merry blur,
I shout, "Hey! Look at my fur!"

Snowflakes swirl like disco lights,
Falling fast on silly sights.
I tumble down, oh what a grace,
A snowman smiles with a frozen face!

Caught in circles, lost in giggles,
I chase my breath while my heart wiggles.
The air is sharp, but spirits high,
Ice-skate dances under the sky!

With a spin and a hop, I make a scene,
Sometimes I'm graceful, sometimes I'm mean.
This frosty playground's such a thrill,
Spinning in circles gives me a chill!

Canine Capers Beneath Snowy Clouds

Paw prints scatter on the ground,
Where excited barks are found.
A fluffy friend with winter zest,
Chasing snowflakes, what a quest!

Through drifts we leap and bounds we take,
Best pals together, make no mistake.
In a snowball fight, who's the boss?
As we tumble, no one is lost!

Their wagging tails, a happy sight,
Catching snowflakes - quite the bite!
In this world of white they thrive,
With every jump, they feel alive!

Under clouds, we race so free,
With canine capers, just you and me.
Laughter echoes in the chilly air,
Beneath snowy clouds, we share our flair!

The Sound of Paws on Ice

Paws tap dance on icy floors,
Like little skaters, on all fours.
With every slip, a yelp and giggle,
It's a winter show, hear them wriggle!

Silver bells the claws make ring,
As they race for joy – let's bling!
Slipping sideways, sliding back,
Ever the star, on this frosty track!

With wags and yips, they glide in style,
Oh, how this icy dance makes us smile!
The sound of paws, a merry tune,
Underneath the cold, beneath the moon!

In a joyful flurry, they prance and play,
On this frozen stage, it's their day.
So come watch the spectacle, quite a slice,
Behold the sound of paws on ice!

Companions in the Cold

Two penguins waddle slow,
One slips, lands in the snow.
Flapping wings, a funny sight,
They laugh so hard, it's pure delight.

Their scarves are bright, sure to clash,
Snowball fights become a splash.
Tumbling down, a frosty cheer,
Warm hearts keep the cold at bay here.

A polar bear, oh what a tease,
Tipsy dance on frozen seas.
"Watch me glide!" he takes a chance,
Ends up stuck in an ice-prone dance.

But hand in hand they seek the sun,
In winter's chill, they still have fun.
Companions true, through thick and thin,
In frozen lands, they always win.

The Hurdles of Antics

A squirrel dreams of endless nuts,
Jumps too high, and now he's stuck.
On a branch, he thinks he's brave,
But now it's just a wobbly wave.

A raccoon joins the hilarious race,
Trips on paws, lands face to face.
"Didn't see that log ahead!"
Squirrel laughs, snorts, and shakes his head.

Down the hill they chase a hare,
Clumsy hops, a wild affair.
With every jump, they lose their grace,
At the finish, it's a funny face.

So when the woods are full of play,
They find new ways to seize the day.
Adventures bloom through every fall,
In friendship's laughter, they have it all.

Sliding Through a Winter's Tale

A snowman dreams of sunny skies,
"Just you wait," he starts to rise.
With a carrot nose all set to glow,
But melting quick as temps do flow.

Two kids race on slippery slopes,
Chasing dreams and grounded hopes.
Face-first land, snow sprays around,
Laughter echoes, a winter sound.

A tiny mouse with boots too big,
Skates around with a confident jig.
Trips and tumbles on the frosty scene,
The cutest blunder you ever seen.

As nightfall wraps the world in white,
Flickering lights twinkle bright.
In winter's tale, they glide and spin,
Creating joy from deep within.

Pawpad Chronicles Under Frozen Canopies

In the woods where snowflakes fall,
Pawprints lead to a snowy ball.
A chatty fox with a frosty grin,
Tells tales of trouble with a whirlwind spin.

A clumsy bear missteps with flair,
Sends snow cascading from the air.
"Oops!" he mumbles, cheeks so pink,
A giant snowball starts to shrink.

Bunnies hop with sass and glee,
Sliding down trees, oh so free!
"Let's build a fort!" they squeal and dash,
Creating a fortress fit for a bash.

Each pawpad writes a tale so bright,
Under frozen stars, they share the night.
With giggles, spills, and icy plays,
These chronicles warm the coldest days.

Our Sliding Symphony on Icy Streets

Oh, winter's grace, the icy flow,
We glide and slip, a comedy show.
With arms flailing wide, we barely steer,
The frozen stage is set, oh dear!

Neighbors watch as we hit the ground,
A chorus of laughter, a joyful sound.
In our icy ballet, we twirl and spin,
A wobbly mishap is sure to win!

Sleds lined up, a makeshift parade,
A symphony played on winter's charade.
With a hill that beckons, we take the ride,
A frosty adventure, come with pride!

As we slide home, feet tangled and cold,
Our winter tales are moments of gold.
Who needs a stage when we have the street?
In this slippery world, we can't be beat!

Musings of a Snowbound Wanderer

Stuck inside with frosty breath,
A cup of cocoa, no sign of death.
Snow covers the ground like a fluffy quilt,
A winter wonderland expertly built.

I dream of sunshine, sand, and sea,
But here I am, a snowed-in spree.
The world outside is a dazzling white,
As I ponder my plight, oh what a sight!

The squirrels are plotting, a heist of seeds,
Gathering goodies for their winter needs.
I watch them dance with a knowing grin,
While I'm moping around in my own snow bin.

What fun I could have in the open air!
Yet here I remain, in my cozy lair.
But wait! A snowball soon may be thrown,
For winter mischief we've brightly sown!

Canine Joys in a Frigid Fairytale

Fido leaps through mounds of snow,
With joy unbounded, he puts on a show.
A tail that's wagging, a heart so free,
In this winter dream, he's pure glee!

He digs for treasures, a hidden bone,
In every pile, he claims his throne.
With a nose so cold and a bark of cheer,
This snowy playground's his frontier!

Snowflakes fall like magical beads,
As he chases shadows, forgetting his deeds.
Bounding through drifts, a comical sight,
In his fairytale of frosty delight.

With a perfect roll and a yawn so grand,
He's on his back, with paws in the land.
In this chilly kingdom, he reigns supreme,
In the world of snow, he's living the dream!

Galloping Through a Dazzling Doldrum

On a horse made of whimsy, we dash and prance,
Through fields of glitter, in a carefree dance.
The winter's grip is a cozy embrace,
We gallop along at a comical pace.

Hooves crunch the snow, a rhythm so sweet,
In a dazzling doldrum, we can't keep our feet.
With hats flying off and scarves in a twist,
Each frosty adventure is too good to miss.

From snowflake to snowman, we play our game,
With giggles and laughter, all feeling the same.
We leap o'er puddles, we tumble and roll,
With hearts full of warmth and joy in the soul.

As the sun sets low, painting skies with pink,
We cherish our moments, we pause, we think.
Onward we ride, our spirits so bold,
In this winter wonderland, our laughter's gold!

Icebound Paths and Whiskered Wonders

On icy paths, I slipped and slid,
Chasing snowflakes, like a crazy kid.
A dog with goggles, quite the sight,
Mixing up left with right all night.

My paws are freezing, I need a drink,
But all I find is snow and stink.
A squirrel laughs, it won't stand still,
I'm the king of winter, but what a thrill!

In the snow, I made a throne,
With legs like sausages, all alone.
The snowman waves but has no sway,
Just another day in winter play.

Finally home, I take a nap,
Dreaming of fields beneath a map.
Icebound paths and whiskered fun,
In my world, I'm always number one.

Struggles in the Snow

Struggling forward, I dig my paws,
Snow flying high; I break the laws.
Every leap feels like a flop,
Oh dear belly, will you ever stop?

I saw a snowman, gave it a nudge,
With all my force, just trying to budge.
It toppled down, what a sight to see,
Now who's the real snowman, me or he?

A snowball fight breaks out with glee,
But they seem to forget about me.
With tail a-wagging, I make a stand,
Get ready for my fluffy snow hand!

So here's to winter, my icy friend,
Every struggle leads to joy in the end.
Through snowy chaos, I dance and sway,
In this frosty world, come what may!

The Tug of Tails

A tug of war with tails so grand,
Squeaky toys fall, it's out of hand.
My buddy pulls, I give a growl,
This fluffy game makes me howl.

Around the house, we dash and dart,
With our tails high, we're off the chart.
Tugging here, and pulling there,
Squealing giggles fill the air.

But oh, what's that? A treat in sight!
Our tails drop low, focus ignites.
No more tugging, now it's a race,
To claim the prize, we pick up pace!

In the end, we share with flair,
A teamwork moment, without a care.
For in this game, the best prevail,
A happy ending and trusty tails!

Canine Capers on a Frigid Trail

On a trail so frosty, I frolic and bound,
Each leap feels epic, with joy profound.
My ears flopping wildly, I smell the air,
Canine capers without a care!

Snowflakes tumble, a frosty delight,
Every gust of wind feels just right.
Down the hills, I zoom and glide,
A fluffy comet with tail spread wide!

I spot a friend with a wagging tail,
We race together, leaving a trail.
With paws in sync, like superheroes,
We conquer the cold, as everybody knows!

At sunset, we bask in twilight glory,
Our joyous romp is a furry story.
Canine capers on this frigid trail,
In winter's embrace, we will never fail!

Pawprints in the Frost

We strolled through winter's chill,
My dog's paws danced on the hill.
With every step, a print appeared,
A masterpiece, or so he cheered.

His breath was foggy, like a cloud,
He pranced around, oh so proud.
But with each leap, he took a dive,
Into the snowdrifts, oh, what a jive!

The neighbors laughed, they had a view,
As he rolled around, tail wagging too.
"I'm a snowball!" he seemed to say,
While I kept shouting, "Come back! Stay!"

Finally, tired, he lay like a lump,
Covered in snow, a fluffy thump.
I took a pic, my phone it shook,
Pawprints in frost, don't judge the rook!

Slippery Adventures on Leash

We headed out, leashes in hand,
But snow and ice had other plans.
With each step, I skated around,
While my pup thought it was all profound.

He zigged and zagged, a furry blur,
While I clung tight, a flailing stir.
One little slip, and off I go,
Straight into a pile of fluffy snow!

He jumped right up, eyes full of glee,
"Look, Mom, the slide's just for me!"
I laughed so hard, the penguins fled,
As I watched my dog launch ahead.

Through slippery paths and frosty fun,
This leash adventure had just begun.
We may have slipped, but it's all okay,
Laughing out loud on a snowy day!

Chasing Shadows in a Winter Wonderland

Beneath the streetlamp's golden glow,
My pup chased shadows, high and low.
He darted left, then quickly right,
In his mind, he was a fearless knight.

"Watch out!" I called, as he took flight,
Bounding forth into the snowy night.
A shadow of a bunny, oh so sly,
He barked and leaped, "Catch that guy!"

But all he caught was a snow-laden flake,
Pouncing and rolling, for goodness' sake!
He shook it off, with a sassy spin,
"Next time, I swear, I'm gonna win!"

In this winter wonderland of white,
Chasing shadows brought pure delight.
We laughed until our cheeks were red,
Hand in paw, with adventures ahead!

The Furry Companion's Expedition

Off we went, my pup and I,
On a wild adventure, under the sky.
He sniffed each tree and chased the breeze,
While I tried hard to keep up with ease.

Through snowflakes swirling, we marched with cheer,
Every rustle made him perk his ear.
"Is it a squirrel?" I humorously guessed,
He dashed away, fully possessed!

The world was white, a fluffy sight,
He rolled and tumbled, pure delight.
I laughed aloud at his furry plights,
As he aimed for snowballs as thrilling bites.

Together we journeyed, side by side,
Into the winter's frosty wide.
My furry friend, my loyal mate,
In every escapade, we celebrate!

Chilly Whirlwinds of Joy

Snowflakes dance with giggles,
As I trip on my own feet,
Every slide turns into splatters,
Turning cold air into sweet treat.

Hot cocoa spills in my lap,
While I laugh at my own flub,
Mittens in a tangled flap,
Winter's joke is really hubbub.

Sledding down the biggest hill,
I scream with uncontrollable glee,
But then I hit a frozen sill,
And discover the snow's not just for me!

Chilly whirlwinds swirl around,
Bringing laughter and giddy freeze,
I'm snowbound in joy profound,
Winter's magic brings me to my knees!

Frozen Footsteps in the Park

I wander through the icy park,
With a well-intended aim,
But one step on a hidden ark,
And my dignity's out of the game!

Sneakers squeak on icy ground,
As I slip and do a twirl,
The onlookers perk up, compound,
Is this a dance, or a tumble whirl?

Snowmen nod as I glide past,
With noses made of carrots bold,
If only they knew what I cast,
A performance worth its weight in gold.

Frozen footprints mark my spree,
A path of laughter and cheer,
You'd think I'm a sight to see,
Navigating winter with no fear!

Paws in the Winter Whisper

Fluffy pup in snowflakes swirls,
Chasing after winds that sing,
Paws leave prints like twirly curls,
A winter dance, a floppy fling.

Sniffing at the frozen leaves,
She bounces like an eager ball,
Excited barks make joy believes,
Winter's tale of fun for all.

Snowballs fly, but she prefers,
To chase around my winter gear,
Every leap, a bundle of furs,
As her silly side draws near.

Paws in the winter whisper bright,
Barking tales of frosty cheer,
In the fluff, she brings delight,
Her joy makes all the cold disappear!

Chasing Shadows on Frozen Ground

I chase my shadow, sly and spry,
But it dodges with a wink,
I leap and stumble, oh my, my!
Pretending 'cause I'm on the brink.

Snowmen chuckle as I woo,
With every goofy swipe of air,
They know what I'm trying to do,
But my shadow's gone, I swear!

Step by step, I'm on this quest,
To catch a glimpse of dark surprise,
But my skills are simply not the best,
Too busy laughing at my tries.

Chasing shadows brings me glee,
Though they vanish like a dream,
Winter's game of tag with me,
Forever slipping down the stream!

Gliding Together on Frosty Streets

On frosty streets we glide and sway,
With wobbling feet, we find our way.
A slip, a slide, laughter in the air,
Who knew winter fun would be such a dare?

Snowflakes twirl like a wild ballet,
As dogs chase tails in a frosty fray.
With noses cold and ears all a-flap,
We'll dance on ice, and then take a nap!

Hot cocoa waits, a warm, sweet treat,
While snowmen wave from their chilly seat.
We'll dodge the puddles, give it our best,
Giggling loudly in this winter fest!

Together we'll trot, oh what a sight,
Frosty adventures, pure delight.
So grab your sled, let's race the breeze,
On gliding streets, we'll freeze with ease!

A Dance of Paws and Ice

Paws on ice, we're sliding round,
As canine giggles bounce off the ground.
A twirl, a leap, it's quite a show,
The dance of pups in the winter glow!

The icy surface makes us brave,
But down we go, oh how we wave!
With tails a-wagging, we rise again,
A frosty dance that knows no end!

Snowballs flying, dogs in a race,
Every twist ends with a silly face.
With winter coats and hearts so light,
We'll keep on dancing into the night!

So grab a friend, let's all take flight,
On this icy stage, it feels so right.
The paws may slip, but spirits soar,
A dance of joy; who could ask for more?

Through Crystalline Streets

Through streets of crystal, we trot with pride,
With every step, we slip and slide.
Chasing after snowflakes, tasting the chill,
In our furry coats, we're ready for thrill!

Every corner's a new surprise,
With icy patches and sparkling skies.
Laughter erupts with each little fall,
As we bounce right back, ready for it all!

Neighbors peek out from windows inside,
As we prance and laugh, full of joy and pride.
Snowballs fly, doggy barks ring clear,
In this crystalline world, winter cheer!

With each frosty breath, we chase our dreams,
Through glistening streets, on frozen beams.
The world's a playground, so come and play,
In this winter wonderland, let's laugh all day!

The Glee of a Blissful Bark

The sun peeks through, the snow is bright,
I wag my tail, ready for flight.
Each fluffy flake is a gift from the sky,
With a joyful bark, I'm ready to fly!

Bounding through drifts, I twist and turn,
In this winter wonder, my heart will burn.
With friends all around, we play tag and race,
The glee of a bark, oh what a place!

I chase after shadows in the pale light,
With every leap, my spirit feels bright.
A snowman's laugh echoes with glee,
As we tumble together, just my dog friends and me!

So capture this moment, make it last,
In the frosty air, we're free and fast.
With joyous barks echoing pure bliss,
In this winter tale, there's nothing amiss!

Snowscapes and Tail-Wagging Tunes

In a snowscape so bright and white,
Puppies prance with sheer delight.
They chase snowflakes with all their might,
Tail-wagging songs take flight.

Snowballs fly and pups all cheer,
They roll in drifts without a fear.
A snowy kingdom, oh so clear,
With frosty noses drawing near.

Their little paws make prints like art,
Each frosty leap a snowy dart.
Warming hearts with every part,
These furry friends are purest heart.

So let's laugh and join their game,
In snowy fields, they stake their claim.
Puppy joy, no two the same,
Snowscapes sing their joyful name.

Barking in the Blizzard's Embrace

Through the blizzard, barking loud,
Pups make up a playful crowd.
They leap and slide, so proud and wowed,
In chilly chaos, quite enshroud.

With snowflakes flying in their face,
They frolic round, a wild race.
A slippery slope is their base,
As laughter echoes through the space.

They tumble down, then shake it off,
With joyful barks, they laugh and scoff.
Their fluffy antics, never soft,
In winter's grip, they spin aloft.

So if you find a pup in glee,
Embrace the blizzard, let it be.
Together in wild jubilee,
Barking tunes, so carefree.

Chilling Adventures of a Friendly Furball

A little furball, fuzzy and round,
In the snow, he's glory-bound.
With every leap, he leaves a mound,
Of chilly fluff, he's happiness-found.

Chasing shadows, he wags his tail,
With a goofy grin, he'll never fail.
Through biting winds, he'll set the trail,
Dancing gaily, he'll prevail.

Snowy escapades, oh what a sight,
A nose so cold, but heart so bright.
With every bark, he spreads pure light,
Adventures in snow, a sheer delight.

So bundle up and join him fast,
For frosty fun that's unsurpassed.
With winter joy that seems to last,
Chilling tales of friendship, blast!

A Tush in the Snow

There's a puppy in the snow, oh dear,
With a fluffy tush that brings such cheer.
He dives in drifts without a fear,
Rolling round, snuggly and near.

His little tail wags, bright and spry,
Covered in snow, a frosty pie.
He takes a tumble, oh my oh my,
With a woof and a giggle, he'll fly!

He turns and spins, a snowy dance,
In winter's grip, he takes a chance.
Every leap is a silly prance,
A plushy bum, a furry romance.

So watch him play, you'll giggle too,
A perfect snowball, fresh and new.
With every wiggle, he'll charm you through,
And soon end up with a snowy dew.

Journey into the Brisk Unknown

I set off on a chilly quest,
With snacks and socks to feel my best.
The wind it's howling, oh what fun!
I think I lost my last hot bun.

The map is upside-down, oh dear,
But I'll not quit, I'll persevere!
Adventure calls, so off I trot,
With silly dreams and one lost lot.

I met a squirrel, he gave me a stare,
I offered him peanuts, he didn't care.
He snickered at my winter coat,
And I just hoped it wouldn't float!

The unknown is nice, but here's the thing,
My fingers are cold, they should wear a ring.
So here's to journeys, may they remain,
A laugh, a snack, and a friendly pain!

Furry Friends in a Frosty Frame

In winter's chill we gather 'round,
With furry friends both lost and found.
A cat in mittens, a dog in shades,
They look so sharp—oh how they parade!

A bunny hops on freshly fallen snow,
In a tiny scarf, looking quite dapper, though.
They race and tumble, then take a nap,
While dreams of treats fill their little gap.

The birds wear hats, it's quite absurd,
So much fashion, it's a wonderful blur.
With furry hats, our friends all cheer,
In this frosty frame, we're full of cheer.

So let's join paws, and dance about,
In laughter and joy, there's never a doubt.
Our hearts grow warm as the cold winds play,
With furry friends, it's a perfect day!

Dashing Through a Dazzling Dreamscape

With fluffy clouds and skies of blue,
I dash through dreams, just me and you.
Each step I take, I stumble and fall,
On marshmallow hills, I bounce and sprawl!

Unicorns prance, with rainbows too,
While jellybeans drip from every dew.
A dancing bear in a polka-dot vest,
Says, "Keep it fun! You're doing your best!"

Stars above twinkle, with silly winks,
And each bright moon laughs as it drinks.
I swing on vines made of licorice lace,
In this dazzling dream, I've found my space.

So let us dash, twirl, and play,
In this clouded wonder, we'll forever stay.
With giggles and joy, let's lose our way,
In a dazzling dreamscape, all night and day!

Watching the Snowflakes Dance With Me

I sit by the window, sipping my tea,
As snowflakes swirl, they dance with glee.
Each flake's unique; it tickles my nose,
Like tiny ballerinas in winter prose.

Outdoors it's cold, but here I stay warm,
Wrapped in my blanket, secured from harm.
The flakes go outside, whirling in flight,
While I munch cookies, what a delight!

They spin and twirl, oh what a show,
I cheer them on, "Go, snowflakes, go!"
They answer back with a soft little kiss,
Each landing on me feels like bliss.

So let them dance, with grace and flair,
While I stay cozy in my fluffy chair.
Together we celebrate, cold and free,
Watching those snowflakes dance with me!

The Icy Waltz of the Wanderer

In snow boots fancy, I glide and twirl,
My dog, the partner, gives a joyful whirl.
We slip and slide in a frosty trance,
Two clumsy dancers in a winter dance.

The penguins watch with a quizzical gaze,
As I stumble forth in this icy maze.
My hat flies off, takes a chilly dive,
While my pup chases snowflakes, oh so alive!

We pretend it's graceful, this winter ballet,
But we both know it's a slapstick display.
With frozen noses, our laughter will ring,
In this frosty waltz, we are the snowy kings!

So here's to the winter, the slips, and the falls,
To cozy hot cocoa and snowball brawls.
With each frosty step and each icy shout,
We'll dance this wild waltz without a doubt!

Paws on Parade through Nature's Crystals

Through fields of white, my pup leads the way,
With paws on parade, in a snow-filled display.
A frosty tiara of crystals so bright,
She prances like royalty, oh what a sight!

Each paw print a masterpiece, oh so neat,
Making snow angels with every little feat.
While I trip and tumble, she barks with glee,
In this winter wonderland, she's fancy and free!

The squirrels shake their heads, puzzled and bold,
As my dog rolls in snow, her coat turning cold.
Squeaky snow toys are strewn all around,
And laughter erupts at the joy that we've found!

With nature's crystals sparkling like stars,
We're bounding through flurries, forgetting our scars.
So here's to a day of park fun and play,
With paws on parade, come join our display!

Spirited Leaps in a Frosty Field

In a frosty field, with a hop and a skip,
My dog takes the lead, on a snow-coated trip.
With marvelous leaps, she defies gravity,
As I stumble behind, a sight of hilarity!

She bounds through the drifts like a furry spring lamb,
While I chase her down, feeling quite like a ham.
Each leap turns to laughter, each slip a delight,
As we frolic together in the pure winter light.

With snowflakes a-flying, she twirls like a pro,
While I try to capture her agility flow.
But my wintery clumsiness steals the show,
As I flail like a fish on the ice, oh no!

In this frosty field, we share joyous yells,
Two silly adventurers, casting winter spells.
So we leap and we laugh, with hearts full of cheer,
In this spirited dance, our fun draws near!

Glistening Trails of Canine Laughter

In the glistening trails of snow, we roam,
With my dog leading, we feel right at home.
Her laughter soars high in the crisp, chilly air,
As we race through the woods, without a care.

The sun sparkles down, a magical charm,
With each little leap, she avoids any harm.
But I trip on a root, what a glorious fall!
And she turns with a grin, as if saying, 'Not at all!'

We leap and we tumble, creating our path,
With snow-covered giggles that spark endless laughs.
The trees join the fun, with branches like arms,
As they sway to the rhythm of winter's sweet charms.

In this snowy wonderland, joy takes the stage,
With glistening trails of laughter, we engage.
So here's to the winter, the fun yet to come,
With my canine companion, we'll always be numb!

Chasing the Sun on a Frozen Day

I woke up this morning, the sun was a tease,
It hid behind clouds, like it's trying to freeze.
I bundled up tightly, like a burrito wrap,
But my nose is still chilly, what a funny mishap!

I pranced to the window, full of bold cheer,
Only to find snowflakes waltzing near.
I shouted at sunlight, 'Come out, don't delay!'
But it winked from afar, enjoying the play.

I danced with my shadow, we jumped like a hare,
Chasing the sunlight, gasping for air.
It's just a frozen day, but I won't wear a frown,
I'll chase it 'til sunset, I'll claim this cold town!

Like penguins on parade, I slip and I slide,
But laughter is warm, it's my sunny inside.
Though the sun may be shy, I'll give it a call,
Chasing the sun on a frozen day—might just win it all!

Skating on Ice with Four-Legged Friends

I took my ice skates, all shiny and bright,
My furry friends joined, what a hilarious sight!
We wobbled and giggled, all over the place,
As my dog tried to skate, he just couldn't keep pace!

My cat wore a helmet, a sight to behold,
She skated in circles, so graceful and bold.
But just when she showed off a fancy little spin,
She slipped on a puddle—oh, how we did grin!

The rabbits hopped loudly, across the cold sea,
Spinning like whirlwinds, as happy as can be.
While I took a tumble, and landed so snug,
My dog leaped beside me—a furry warm hug!

With giggles and barks, we skated till night,
The stars twinkled down, such a magical sight.
In laughter we rolled, four-legged delight,
Skating on ice with my friends, what a night!

The Frostbitten Expedition

Our frostbitten quest began with a cheer,
We hopped through the snowdrifts, full of good cheer.
With mittens all fluffy, we waved at the cold,
But every step forward resembled a mold!

We packed some hot cocoa, it spilled on my head,
My friends laughed so hard, they fell back instead.
The snowman we crafted, a creature so grand,
Gave me a snowball—oh, isn't it grand?

With toes that were frozen, and noses that glowed,
We trekked through the snow, following our road.
But the map was quite shaky, my compass was lost,
We circled in circles, at quite a high cost!

Yet laughter kept bubbling, like a hot pot of stew,
Though frostbite was creeping, we still pushed on
through.
With rosy red cheeks and feet that were sore,
Our frostbitten adventure was something to adore!

Leash Tugging

My dog and I ventured on a snowy trail,
With leash tugging wildly, I followed the veil.
He spotted a squirrel, and I lost my grip,
We danced in a frenzy, what an epic trip!

The leash turned to spaghetti, in a game of tug-of-war,
I stumbled and giggled—oh, how I adore!
He leaped like a champion, full of pure glee,
While I tried to keep up, but oh, let me be!

As we twirled through the snow, I questioned my fate,
Was it me walking him, or him guiding the gait?
But together we laughed, a sight to behold,
A duo in motion, both silly and bold!

With snowflakes a-flying, our antics en masse,
We frolicked on pathways, nothing could surpass.
So if you see us, just know this is true,
In leash tugging fun, our friendship just grew!

Daydreaming in Snow

The world turned to white, like a giant soft cake,
I laid down in snow; a snow angel I'd make.
As I stared at the clouds, a daydream took flight,
Imagining snowmen, all dancing tonight!

Robots with snowballs were battling great kings,
While penguins in tuxedos were practicing swings.
A polar bear chef was baking with cheer,
All in my daydream, besides me right here!

Yet as I drifted, a snowflake popped by,
It landed right on me—oh, how I did sigh!
"Dear friend," it exclaimed, with a twinkle so bright,
"Join in my frolic, it's pure winter delight!"

So we rolled in the snow, creating a scene,
While unicorns giggled, all merry and keen.
In daydreaming snow, the magic ignites,
In worlds far and wide, this winter invites!

Meandering in a White Wonderland

Snowflakes land on my nose,
I trip and shout, "Oh no, it shows!"
With every slip, I'm full of glee,
A snowman rolls off, just like me.

The kids scream loud, they throw their balls,
While I keep falling, hear my calls!
A snowball fight turns into chaos,
I find a drift—oh what a loss!

My hands are cold, my cheeks are pink,
I ponder snow, do cows really drink?
I chase my hat, it takes a flight,
Into a bush, what a silly sight!

As snowmen melt, we wave goodbye,
With frosty laughter, oh my my!
We'll meet again, you snowy ground,
When winter's back, fun will abound!

Boundless Energy

I wake up bright, the sun is high,
With boundless energy, I could fly!
I leap from bed, like a rocket's launch,
To dance around, the world I'll haunch!

A coffee pot brews, but I'm too fast,
I buzz and whirl, I'm out to blast!
My friends all yawn while I jump and jig,
"Hey, slow down, you joyful twig!"

I bounce like rubber, can't sit still,
They question my breakfast; it's just pure will!
With twirls and skips, I conquer the day,
"Where's the rest of you?" they often say.

But when the sun dips low and night creeps in,
I drop to the couch, it's clear I can't win!
A zany blast now takes a rest,
But come tomorrow, I'll rise like the best!

Frozen Ground

The path is slick, with frosty sheen,
One false move, and down I lean!
My feet go flying, 'tis a slip and slide,
I find new ways to take a ride!

I channel my inner ice skater,
But fall flat, like a bad actor!
A dog goes past, it gives me a look,
As if to say, "Hey pal, you shook?"

Snowball fights turn into big spills,
I toss a throw, but it's full of thrills!
I sow confusion, what a round,
On this slippery, frozen ground!

Yet laughter rings out, all in good jest,
This frosty fall turns into a quest!
With every slip, giggles abound,
In the midst of this frosty playground!

Adventures of the Four-Legged Friend

My dog just spotted a squirrel so sly,
He leaps and bounds, oh my, oh my!
His tail a whirlwind, a sight to behold,
As nature's comedy starts to unfold.

He digs in the snow, all paws and paws,
Uncovering treasures and more furry flaws.
With a leap and a bark, he charges ahead,
While I stand back, just shaking my head!

In puddles he jumps, oh mud, what a blast!
He rolls on the ground; it's a dirty cast!
A quick bath awaits, oh how he shall love,
The shower will come as a gentle shove.

But back he comes, all clean and bright,
Ready for mischief, under the moonlight!
Each adventure we share, a twist on the bend,
With my four-legged buddy, the fun never ends!

Blurring Lines Between Fun and Friction

The ice rink calls, I lace my skates,
But first I wobble—it's slippery fates!
I try to glide, but instead I fall,
Like a clumsy penguin, I'm losing it all!

My friends all cheer, they giggle and point,
I'm waving my arms, I've lost my joint!
A spin, a glide, it turns into flop,
With every move, I feel like a mop!

A race to the end, I'm face to the ground,
My dignity's lost, where's the fun I found?
But laughter erupts, it's better this way,
In a world where we slip and slide through the fray!

So let's dance on the ice, give it one more try,
With smiles and slips, we'll reach for the sky!
Though fun and friction may blur their design,
My heart leaps for joy, in this frosty shrine!

A Tailspin on Icy Terrain

I stepped out on the ice so bright,
But slipped and spun with all my might.
My breakfast landed on a tree,
As squirrels laughed and mocked at me.

I grabbed my dog, he took the lead,
He thought it fun, I felt the speed.
We twirled around, quite like a dance,
While onlookers stared, holding their pants.

The neighbors chuckled at my plight,
"Is that a person or a kite?"
But in the end, with coats and tails,
We left behind our icy trails.

So if you're bold and feeling spry,
Just watch your step or say goodbye.
For icy paths can be a thrill,
But laughter is the greatest chill.

Taking the Scenic Stumble

I thought I'd take a stroll today,
With all this snow, what could go astray?
But down I went, a graceful flop,
Like some old rag doll in a shop.

The snowflakes danced around my head,
As I sprawled out, I thought I'd fled.
A family giggled from their slope,
While I was busy losing hope.

I tried to get up, my boots betrayed,
The ice below was well displayed.
Then off I rolled like a big ol' bear,
Creating a snowman, unaware.

But laughter filled the air with glee,
As I became a sight to see.
If life's a stumble, take it in stride,
And enjoy the joy that snowflakes provide.

Snowflakes and Wagging Tails

My dog is out, he loves the snow,
With leaps and bounds, he steals the show.
He wiggles and barks, a furry delight,
While I trip over as he takes flight.

The snowflakes swirl, they kiss his nose,
He catches them all, like tiny prose.
But as he bounds, I lose my grip,
And down I go—now it's a trip!

He turns around, wags his tail,
As I recover from my fail.
Together we play, a lovely chase,
Forget about my snowplow face.

Life's better with a pup, it's true,
Even if they make you fall anew.
With wagging tails and snowy days,
We laugh and play in joyful ways.

Adventures in the Chill

Let's gear up for an icy spree,
With gloves and hats, just you and me.
But as we march, a snowball flew,
'Twas my own cousin, who else but you?

The laughter echoed through the park,
As everyone tried to make a mark.
But not before a slip and slide,
Where I did tumble, my butt did glide.

A snowman formed from all my flops,
With carrot nose and boots as props.
I found a hat that's quite absurd,
And now I'm famous, have you heard?

So join the fun, don't stay inside,
Embrace the chill and take the ride.
For winter's magic is a thrill,
And laughter echoes through the chill.